THE
CONFIDENT
WOMAN
GUIDE BOOK

THE
CONFIDENT
WOMAN
GUIDE BOOK

CONCETTA FERLISI

authorHOUSE®

AuthorHouse™ LLC
1663 Liberty Drive
Bloomington, IN 47403
www.authorhouse.com
Phone: 1-800-839-8640

Published by AuthorHouse 01/07/2014

ISBN: 978-1-4918-4203-4 (sc)
ISBN: 978-1-4918-4202-7 (e)

Library of Congress Control Number: 2013922388

CONTENTS

CHAPTER 1

STAYING STRONG

Some women go through abuse, torture and pain and don't know what to do. We'll let me tell you, you're not alone. Every woman goes through some kind of pain in their life and don't know how to overcome it. Well, let me tell you something "it's ok" to go through things in life. We all go through hard times and if anyone ever said they haven't well they're lying. You need to believe in yourself and not anyone. Never doubt yourself just because you've been hurt. Take the first step and trust yourself to get through that situation. Even if you feel scared. It's okay because once you empower yourself to move forward without looking back, you are giving yourself the courage to stand as a confident woman. When all others try to abuse you with their words, the best way to overcome it is by not focusing on them too much. You see, sometimes they will say these things to you to hurt you so badly because it's who they really are as a people. They keep everything bottled up inside until they explode and blame other people for their pain. You should always walk away from anyone who is turning you down and making you feel less than a woman because remember you are more than a woman who will not let anybody define who you are. You define yourself and you give yourself the ability to take control over every word they say and turning it into a positive new attitude. Tell yourself, "well, if these things are going on in my life I will not be afraid because these are the things that help you grow as a woman and help you deal with new situations that come along the way." When you wake up in the morning, don't just wake up with so much anger in your heart. Release it with slowly breathing in and exhaling out. Don't think about the past so much because how can you move on in the present moment if you are still worried about everything that happened "let it go". The only thing you can do is get passed it with great confidence by believing in yourself and not worrying about what others have to say about you because what they say has no power over you unless you make them control your thoughts. What I mean by that is, if you believe what they are saying is true then you are giving them a law over your life. Begin by forgiving anyone who has ever hurt you not because they deserve it. You need to learn how to heal yourself with great expectations. Turn your thoughts in your mind to the most positive "I will be ok", "I am ok." "I believe all that I want in life I will achieve and the outcome will be what you believe in." No one can give you that confidence unless you trust yourself first. That is the most important thing to ever do. Who can you trust if not yourself? Believing in yourself is what gets you through life staying strong and moving forward makes you even stronger than you can ever imagine. When you feel like, "well ok, how will I get pass an abusive relationship?" You can get through it by seeking help. Don't just sit behind and let the person who abuse you take that power out of you. When you seek help, you are proving to yourself well ok, "I am going on with my life I am not just letting the past keep eating me up." You already moved on passed that path with a new one. When you are looking for help believe me, there are other people out there in this world who can relate to your problem and help you start your life again. If you stay stuck home and let your life just pass you by the days get longer and the nights get even longer. Everything starts to seem so hard but if you take that first step and help yourself get pass the past pain you are only growing stronger everyday as a woman and you can walk with that confidence. When you look at yourself look at yourself as a woman of great strength. Stand strong in what you believe in as women and don't bring yourself down because of useless words or harsh comments thrown at you. Remember to remind yourself every day, "I am beautiful" "I love who I am", "no one will take that away from me." "No one will take me down because I will not let them control my emotions only I have the power to overcome everything by trusting who I am as a woman." "The matter of the truth is that if I fail I will not let my tears wash away my life I will dry them away and start a new day with a new thought that my life is worth more than anything in this world." When you begin your day think about what is going to be ahead of you and how great life is to you. Turn your focus on believing that you can make it in life. That person that hurt you is the one who is not going to make it life because, they will live with that guilt all of their life even if they don't show you. You shouldn't let them stand in front of you but let them get out of your life and by doing that you take control over every aspect, every hurtful, painful thing that they have ever done to you. When they see you growing stronger as a woman then they will know that they didn't fail you, they couldn't fail you but only empowered you. You are the true winner and moving forward is your only goal in life. Remember, you are something more beautiful than you can ever imagine. What you think does matter, so don't listen to nonsense that comes your way because, the truth of the matter is people are always going to bring you down once they see you are getting past that painful path you were once in. When you put your trust and say well, "I know things will get better for me", you are making yourself so strong and if it feels like you can get pass the pain of the past. Learn how to take it one day at a time by doing that you are taking the pain out of your life little by little. When you begin your day begin it with allowing yourself to have the better in life not the worst. Some woman are so hurt by the past that they find themselves constantly thinking about what happened to them its "ok." You can get through this by talking to someone to help you out. Maybe, what you've been through someone else has been through it to and they can relate to your situation. When you begin to talk to someone you will feel a bit release from whatever, it is that is making you turn back to the past. Start fresh and keep it going, look always at a better path that you might have in life. Do the things you always wanted to do. Believe me it's never too late to do what you want to do. Some, woman have been abused by a lover and they have overcome it with great confidence. "Believe that you can overcome it to and the confidence you always wanted will begin when you begin to trust yourself." Remember, when you think you fail as a person you didn't. Don't let the past impact who you are as a woman. You are going to make it in life even, if you feel like it's going to take forever to start all over again. Things are going to happen in life but, the best way to deal with it is by dealing with it and not just letting it overtake you and bringing you all the way down. Don't ever think that everything you ever dream about or wanted is over its not over "until you say it's over" that's when you bring yourself to a new level and say this is where my life begins this is how my life is going to be. "I will improve myself and not let the past take over me." Pain is only strong if you let it have power over you. You can overcome it with not letting it confuse you as a person because, pain is something that you feel, it's an emotion but what you want is a goal. You can achieve that goal by bringing yourself up and pushing yourself forward, that's what, makes you stronger each and every day. Don't ever say I am alone because you're not. Many women feel like they are because, what they've been through so much, they feel neglected. You are not alone, you will come to a point in life were you will see that there are other women who can relate to your situation. When you come to realize that you will feel more Confident because, you know that there is other woman out there who can help speak to you and tell you that "it's ok." When you begin your days remember to tell yourself "today is a new day, a better brighter calmer day today." "I will be ok and all that I want in my day today I will achieve." See you have to bring in that positive in your heart so your mind will begin to grow strong and that's what will make you a stronger Woman every single day of your life. Remember, You are an Amazing Woman and what you want in your life will be accomplished with great strength that you keep inside. "Keep yourself motivated every single day by staying positive." "Today is the new beginning of your life."

CHAPTER 2

SELF ESTEEM

"Why am I so afraid to be alone? Why can't I do the things I always wanted to do?" Many women question this in their daily life. Well the truth of the matter is you can't do what you want to do because of the lack of self-esteem you contain as a woman. You see as a woman you have to have "self-esteem" and "self-control" to do what you want to do. Even if you feel like you can't. The reason why you're not getting through with what it is that you want is because of your negative thinking. Stop bringing yourself down and give yourself a chance. Once you do that, you are building your self-esteem and growing as a woman of great strength. Never abuse yourself with hurtful words. Where is that going to lead you? Nowhere and nothing that you want will be accomplished because you are bringing more pain into your daily life. Stick with your thoughts of happiness. Some women may question, "well how can I be happy if everything I ever wanted is not turning out the way I would like it to be?" Start thinking about something that you would like to do. Something that makes you happy as a person and continue with that. Don't let no one stop what you always intended to do. Keep that self-esteem. Instead overcome it with a good positive attitude that says, "I can do what it is I want to do", "I just got to believe that I have the power to do it even if it takes me a lifetime." Remember, your life is only beginning. For women who have been hurt, the pain won't last forever. It will leave in time, when you learn how to control every emotion and not let it control you. When you think the goodness of yourself instead of the bad. Then you will begin to see that you changed your ways of thinking and that's what gives you the brightest light inside of your soul. Don't ever turn yourself down. Don't ever think you are not strong enough and just give up. In order to have self-esteem, you must trust in yourself and have courage. Remind yourself to say this out loud, "I am a woman who can define herself and no one will overpower me with their harsh words or actions because I will not let them succeed in life. Instead I will succeed in life." "I will prove to myself that I have great ability in life." You don't need to prove anything to anyone because you are a woman with self-esteem. You will see yourself get through life even if obstacles stand in your way. Why should you be so afraid? Hey, things are going to happen in life and sometimes you can't prevent them from happening but you learn how to build that self-control and how to get on with your life. Life is not a movie. It is the real thing and what is happening in your life is your business and no one else's. So don't think you need to explain your life to anyone because you don't. All you need to do is believe that you were strong enough to survive what you've been through and where you stand now is because of the strength that you carried with you inside. That's when you think you lost self-esteem but what you just did was gain it. Pain and hurt made you a stronger more empowering woman now in this present moment. You can do all things when you focus on yourself. Words are painful but that shouldn't bring you down. People are always going to talk so let them say whatever it is that they want to say because if you pay attention to them then it means you believe them. If you ignore them and don't pay any attention to what they say then you are the woman who has the ability and the strength to move past your worst enemy. You see some women think what other people say are true or going to happen to them. Nonsense, they are foolish and very immature they don't even know themselves or what it is that they are saying to you because they are confused as a person. You see, what they have going on in their life is less and what you have going on in your life is everything they ever wanted. That's why you should control your emotions and you will see yourself gain that self-control. When you do that the person that sees that will know that they have no power, no effect on you and there words are useless. When they see you moving forward in life they will stop there nonsense because they see that they can never win over you or anything that you do. Some women find there life to be too complicated to say that they have self-esteem. If you don't give yourself credit for anything in your life, then guess what? You are not giving yourself a chance in life. Turn to love yourself. Respect yourself because if you don't know how to respect yourself you lose self-control. Think of yourself as the person you always knew you would be. Look at the very present moment and tell yourself from here on I move only up and not down. Bring that self-love into your heart. Complete it with trusting all your emotions and letting go of the things that you think are bringing you down. The woman you are is the woman you define yourself as and if you don't let people treat you with respect then you are letting them gain that power over your life. A woman who defines her own self is a great woman of power and strength. Don't ever think, "well I can't be positive about myself, I am not that kind of person." Nonsense, if you truly believe in yourself and love yourself you will think positive about yourself. Remember, the past can't affect you unless you let it remain with you always. The past Is the past and you can't go back and erase it even though you wish you could and never had to go through what you did. Don't question yourself so much. Just leave everything where it was and move on with a new beginning, a new page in your life. You can begin. You can change yourself. Get yourself focused on what really matters in your heart and continue on with life. Life is never going to be a cup of wine and a piece of cheesecake but its life and every woman has to go through something in life. They must always remain in control of themselves. You have to have self-esteem because that is the most important thing in a woman's life. No woman should be without it. Every woman should know that they are in control of their mind, their body, their emotions and most importantly there life. Nobody has the right to bring you down. Some people just don't have common sense and will always be that way because they grew up with those kinds of values. It's up to you if you will let them overpower you and the answer is? "No." You will not let the enemy win. They will lose in all that they try to do to you. When you look in the mirror look at all the beauty that you see, all the love that you represent and keep that in mind with you every day. When you are going out to work or just out. With that being said, I am sure you will see that you will gain more control of the aspects in your daily life. You will learn to live with great values and positive outcomes in your life. Some women will feel less confident about the things they don't have because they see other woman who have it. Just because someone has more than you, you shouldn't allow that to destroy who you are. Who you are is just fine. Everybody has a different plan in life and if you don't see yourself feeling happy then change your life around. Do something that will lift you up or something that will make you happy in life. Do something that you always wanted to do and don't let anything get in your way or confuse you. Start from the very bottom and work yourself all the way up to the top and you will see yourself improving. You will gain so much more control over your life. Things will start to work out for the best in your life. You are your own person no one can take your self-control away from you unless you make them take it away. Always look at your life as a new beginning. Tell yourself these are the things I want to achieve and believe that you will make them come true. Why should you not believe in yourself? Others don't have the power to control you. When they speak like that it's because they must have failed at something in life that they thought they would have accomplished. They have lost all of their strength and faith in themselves. Don't let them do that to you just because they had that done to them. Instead, improve your situation for the better and sometimes just by taking the first step all on your own. That's when you will see yourself beginning your future and the outcome will be so beautiful. You will be amazed on how much has change in your life and the reason for that is because you gave yourself a second chance in life. You were the one who believed in yourself and believed that you were going to overcome all of the obstacles that were in your way. Some women don't believe that they will have many changes in their life even when they try. Once again lack of self-esteem. You can't do that to yourself. You must always believe in yourself. Normally, things sometimes don't work out the way you want. Well maybe it's because it wasn't meant to be. That shouldn't stop you from trying again, should it? "Absolutely not". You should never ever stop trying to do what you dream of doing. That is the second most important part of self-esteem. Self-Esteem begins by moving through the deepest path and to watch your-self enter a new road ahead. You can do it. No as a matter of fact, you will do it. You will see all will end well. Remember, you are in control so take control and watch yourself be so empowered by the new things that are beginning in your life. Your life will begin to blossom like a beautiful rose because you have grown so much with that self-esteem and a woman of great strength. You are going to make it in life and its ok if it takes some time. Things take time. It's ok if you feel like it's taking a while to go the way you want them to go. Just remember, take it one day at a time and watch your life begin to change. A woman who can do all that she ever wanted to do and never gives up on herself is a woman who hasn't lost her ability of loving herself. See you can get passed the pain. You can see a new path way in life because when you walked away from the past emotions you gave yourself a change in life. So keep on going and remember you can show yourself how much you truly care about your life when you don't give up on yourself.

CHAPTER 3

TRUSTS

When you've had a hurtful and painful past it's extremely hard to trust anyone and it's even harder to let them in your life. To trust someone all over again is like learning how to drive a car if you don't be careful it might lead you back into that same painful path you were once in. Let me help you how to begin to trust someone. Not everyone is going to hurt you, not everyone is going to be negative towards you. Trust slowly and begin by giving a person a chance in life. Don't be so negative on that person because of what another person may have done to you. Let yourself begin by taking a risk and allowing yourself to trust because you will begin to see how you are changing as a woman and beginning to not let the past interfere with your future. Don't be so judgmental and don't criticize anyone for what you have been through. Why is it that some women feel like everyone is out to get them when they have been hurt? I will tell you why. It's because the person that hurt you in life has taken your ability to trust. They made you feel worthless and not able to move through a new phase in life. Don't let them stop you from trusting others. When a person tries to be friends with you give them a chance. Don't be so quick to push them out. Don't let the past people affect your present moment. You are much stronger than whatever it is that a certain person has put you through. Once you gain yourself, trust you will begin to see how easy it is to trust others. Enroll yourself in a program, a class or groups were you can get to talk to people and be social while having other people surrounding you. Always begin a new day every-day. Remember, you are creating your own chapter to your story. You are the author of your life and no one else. You are the one who can say, "I will begin to trust again. Just because I have been hurt doesn't mean I have to let that affect me for the rest of my life." Tell yourself, "I am a new woman today. My day begins by empowering myself to trust others as I would want them to trust me." Some women have a hard time committing to the word trust. Trust is something you gain. It doesn't come over night. You must learn how to trust even if you had a difficult past. It's a new beginning when someone says the word trust and it's also very hard to trust when you don't even know that person. You shouldn't judge everyone just because someone did something hurtful to you in your life. You should learn how to give someone a chance. If you meet a new friend or new lover, give them a chance because not everyone is out to get you. You shouldn't be scared to trust again. I mean it's normal to feel a little nervous but not to the point where you feel like the only person you want in your life is just yourself. It's really not healthy at all. Loneliness hurts. To get past that, begin to trust other people. If you can't, then it is ok to get group counseling which will help you improve your past pain that you are going through in life. One way or another, you will have to do something to help yourself. If not, when will you ever begin to trust others? If not others then who? You can get passed things in life that seem so hard. It just takes some time in life. Some things may seem to be so hard for you at this point but one thing is for sure it won't last forever unless you open up a new chapter in your life and begin. Take a piece of paper and write down all the things you use to be like and how you use to trust. Take it from there one step at a time. When you go over the list, you will come to reach a point where you will see that in one time in your life you trusted someone. Then someone negative took that trust away from you. So why is it still affecting you now right now at this present moment? If you have any questions, you should ask yourself "why am I letting it affect me till this day?" You should start to state the facts of the past and see how everything was. Once you overcome this you must start with a new focus and a new positive attitude. You can move forward. You can start again and you can begin your life as stating the fact, "I will not let my past define me and who I am as a woman. I will define myself as a woman who can do all great things with that trust that I have always had in life. No one will ever steal that trust away from me. I trust myself as the person I am and all that I will one day become." What you need to do is not be afraid of who you are. Whatever it is that any person has put you through, don't be terrified to stand up for yourself. Speak your mind. Give yourself the courage to live beyond anything that stands in your way of confusing you as a person. People may have hurt you badly and they may have even taken so much from you because of what they put you through. Do not let them steal your goals or your dreams. Step away from the past issues and begin with a new pattern in life. You don't want to make the person who brought you down gain all power over you. Remember, no one can control you. Only you control yourself in all that you do in your life. Even if you had friends in the past that have betrayed you or hurt you and turn their backs on you. You may feel like not trusting new people because of what happened to you back then. Why would you let that person continue to affect your life? You can get past anything by allowing yourself to be a powerful woman with a strength that goes beyond your limits. The best way in life to get past it is by encouraging yourself to not be afraid of taking risks, moving past that pain and meeting new people. It doesn't mean that you have to trust them all in one day. It just means that you get to know who they are as a person and you take it from there one step at a time. Sometimes, you might even come to realize that what you've been through somebody has been through almost the same exact thing. Together you can build a friendship and begin to see that certain trust is coming back into your life. Trust has to always begin by trusting yourself and who you see yourself as a person. When you feel neglected or abused from someone you may have met in the present moment, then you know the best thing is not to start a friendship with them and just walk away. Start moving on in your life because you don't want to bring yourself back down the same road. You want to lead yourself to a road were you will be full of success and you can look back in time and feel proud of yourself that you've accomplished the greatest thing in your life. Once you begin to trust yourself and empower yourself every day, you will see how you have given yourself the chance that you thought was impossible. Believe me, it is never impossible to start over again in life. You have to be the woman who is willing to change. When you see that you are willing to change, your happiness will begin to grow and all of your trust will begin to come back to you. When you trust, it doesn't mean that you take that first step and trust someone all the way when you just met them. It means take it slow and one day at a time to get to know who they really are and what there all about. Some women want to feel safe about themselves when they are meeting new people and that is ok because that is the beginning of your path of taking the risk to start all over again and trusting yourself to be strong enough. If someone may have hurt you so much that they may have even taken away your courage as a person to believe that other people are able to come into your life then why would you let anyone who has done you wrong in life turn your life around? Don't ever let anyone think they can do that to you. "No Way." Remind yourself every day, "why would I give any person any power over my mind and my thoughts of living as the woman I intend to live as"? There are many women who just lose all of their confidence because of what an abusive man may have done or said to them. Why would "he" the man that has hurt you, be able to bring you down? No man should ever have any power over any women because that is not a man but a coward. Don't let a man stand in your life and try to take complete control over who you are as a woman. Don't let him define you because you don't want to be in that type of pain and humiliation. What you want to do is get past it by saying, "you know what, you're not worthy of being in my life and trying to take my self-trust away from me. "I believe that I am a woman who doesn't need to be abused by any man. Any man that does those things to a woman is not a real man". Believe me you'll see what a real man is when he enters your life. He will treat you like a princess and not make you be afraid of trusting yourself and loving who you are as a woman. He won't define you but love you as the woman you are. Anytime you feel hurt you can overcome it but it's all up to you. It's all in your mind if you think you can get past that pain. Think of yourself every day and say, "ok, today is the day I will improve myself. I will be ok, why should I look back at the past so much"? When you keep on looking back at the past then guess what you are giving the person who hurt you the power to take all of your control away from you. Why should they have all of their self-esteem as a person and you as a woman in pain because of what you have experience? You need to know that you will be worth more than anything and no pain is worth taking away your ability as a woman. As a woman you should be able to feel that you can be a woman who is able to trust. If you trust yourself, how could anyone in the world hurt you? They can't. You believe in yourself and you continue to see yourself as a woman with the strength as strong as ever can be. Trusting might be like going on a rollercoaster but once you keep going on then you'll realize, "hey it's really not that bad. I can trust." You should trust most importantly. Never let anyone say that they had all of that power over your life because they feel like they took an inch of your life away from you. No one should be able to take your ability away from your life.

CHAPTER 4

LOVE

Love is the strongest word in the world. It's almost as sweet as the taste of wine. Love is a feeling that goes beyond deep. Loving yourself is the first priority in life before you love anyone else. When you receive love, it should be true. There should be no pain in the word love because in love that word pain does not exist. Every woman deserves to be loved. Most women fall out of love, have abusive relationships or end up with painful divorces and it's very hard for them to love again. That is very understandable. Love will find you again. I want you to know that, even if you don't think that you will ever love again you will. Someone is out there. Someone special is searching for you but still hasn't found you and when they do you will fall back in love. That person will bring you to a whole new level on the path of love and you won't ever look down on love again. Love is a very powerful thing. It goes deeper than you think. It's an aspect that reaches your heart and soul and it can only be found when you are ready to love again. It doesn't mean you have to go out looking for love. Love will find you when you least expect it. Some women question, "why is love so hard to find"? Well, it's because of what so many men have been through too in their lives. They may have been hurt, scared or even just not ready to be in a relationship. When love does find you, give it a chance. Don't just walk away from it because of what you may have been through in the past. Let me ask you this, do you think the person who hurt you would want you to be in a relationship, a real healthy loveable relationship? My answer is "No". So, why should you let them take that part of your life away from you? Receive that love because you deserve to be loved and to give love. No man is worth all of that pain. If you're in a relationship that is abusive "Get Out Now". He doesn't love you. He is hurting you in so many levels, emotionally and physically. "Get out" and "Stay out" and continue with your life. There is someone out there who is truly going to love you. Even if it takes a while for you to receive that love, he is out there. Just give yourself a chance to move past the pain that you carry with you every day. Here is another thing every women should know, to love, I mean truly love and be loved you must have courage. You must have the strength inside of you to believe that love is what you truly want. Have the courage to know you can accept it without asking any questions. Love is more than a word and it's a deep feeling that you feel when your heart is pumping through your veins. Don't question yourself about what a man should need from you because any man that keeps on needing is a man who thinks he is in control of you. What you need is a man who will be able to give the love you always deserved. I do believe love should be fair. It shouldn't hurt and it shouldn't be hard to live with. Some women who start a relationship with a man instantly say, "this is the one. I know I can feel it". I say, "Oh Please! How can you feel it if you don't even know that person yet?" Get to know that person a little better before you jump to consultations because the only thing you can know is maybe he might be the right one for you because you might have things in common. Guess what? When you find the man that you have always been looking for make sure he treats you with respect because if he doesn't then he thinks he's the one in control of you. No man should be in control of any woman they love but they should only be in love with them. Love is a word that contains more than just L.O.V.E. It's a commitment, a new path in life. With that being said, you should know the most beautiful thing in the world is to have love and be loved unconditionally. When you meet someone, don't be so quick to say to them "I love you" because you might scare them away. Give them some time to get to know you and to know who you are as a person. When it's the right moment and right place you won't be afraid to open up and tell that person how you truly feel about them. You must always allow that person to express themselves to you. It shouldn't always be all about you. Once you see that special someone in your life is making your heart beat fast, taking you to places you always wanted to go and you can share anything with that person, then you begin by allowing all of your love to grow for that certain man in your life. You will see his love for you begin to grow as well. What you have been through in the past doesn't have to affect you from receiving love. Why wouldn't anyone want to love you? Is it because of what happened to you in your past? Your past is your business and nobody else's. You should never be ashamed of who you are or what you have been through because you are more than just pain. You are loved and you should never let anyone tell you different. Your life is only beginning. What you feel is your emotions. You should always love yourself even if you don't think that anyone loves you because you are wrong. Love is more than a word. It's the deepest feeing you can ever feel. Love begins in your heart and if you love yourself then that is the biggest part of you approving of yourself. You don't need to have loved in order to be loved. Only loving yourself is what should be the first thing in your life. You only have to love yourself to gain that self-trust. Many women say, "well I don't believe in true love it doesn't exist?" Some women say, "love means nothing to me because I have never had a man love me and show me that they truly cared for me." Well, why would you think less of yourself? Just because you are not loved by a man? A man is not the only thing in this world that is supposed to give you love. Love can come from all aspects of life such as friends, family, animals and much more. Why would you feel like, "well hey I am nothing without the love from a man"? Nonsense, you are a woman who will not be afraid to say, "I love myself first and that's what's important". Don't be so harsh on yourself. Don't judge yourself just because you are not in a relationship. Some women find it hard to love themselves when they are not loved by a man. They feel like they don't matter and nothing in this world is important to them but only to be loved by a man. Some women will see others in a relationship and feel like, "why is it that I am not loved"? "Why can't I have that same kind of love and be in a relationship"? Many women do not understand the aspect of what love really represents. Love comes at the right moment not overnight. What other women have, you shouldn't compare yourself to them. Your life is your life and their life is their life. Never look at someone else's life and wish to have what they have because you need to value what you already have and what you will continue to have one day. You need to know that you are worth more than anything in this world. Don't be so hard on others and don't judge them for what they have. Just stay focused on yourself and you will see that things will get much better when you least expect it. Well, some women also question, "how will I know what love is if I have been so hurt"? "How can I know if any man will really love me"? When you meet someone and they welcome you into their life with open arms, accept you, understand every point of view, and are attentive to you that's when they respect you and show you that they care for you. They would do anything for you. See, when a man tries to better you and helps you to move on from your past or helps you overcome some of the things that you are still holding on to then you will know that this man in your life is doing all of these things for you because he truly cares. If he didn't he would have just walked away in the very beginning. That's when you know that he is bringing the positive in your life. To help you have a new attitude about yourself. Not every man will have the qualities you are looking for but they may be the right person for you. They will be with you and love you unconditionally and always treat you the way you always wanted to be treated. Don't be so hard on a man for what you may have experienced with another man. They are not the same person. You see, sometimes we think that if one man hurts us then all men will. This is not true. There are plenty of men who are willing to give you their heart. Meaning they are willing to climb the highest mountain do anything you ever wanted to do but just didn't know how to do it. When you get to understand yourself and trust yourself to get over the past then you are beginning a great new path in your own life. Life is beautiful and the things that you want in life are up to you on how you would like to reach up to them. Don't just say, "well, I don't know how to reach up to them" and just begin to bring yourself down. Trust me; just stop stressing yourself because you may meet a man who will show you what a real man is about and not a clown that was in your past. You are worth more than any pain. If you do begin dating and you don't like what you see then just walk away and start fresh again. There is no need to keep on holding on to someone that will never love you or show you that they don't care for you. If a man is constantly coming up to you when he sees you and is trying to talk to you give him a chance. If a man is willing to give you all of his love and continues to chase you then you will see that's real love. If you see that this man is trying to be with you, give him a chance and don't walk away because you may see how much that man can prove to you that he truly loves you and how much he cares about you. So why should you give up on love? Is it because love gave up on you in the past? Think about it. Are you willing to make the past effect you from receiving true love? Are you going to define the present with a new beginning saying, "this is my time", "my right", "my life and am going to live it to the fullest", or "I am never going to doubt myself anymore for any other man who has tried to destroy me?" You need to tell yourself, "I am going to move on in this new path of my life and live it in the most righteous way ever."

CHAPTER 5

SLOW IT DOWN

Okay well, here is your new beginning in your life. It doesn't mean now that you found true love or that you are reaching something that you want to do in life that makes you happy like a career, that you have to hurry up and rush things. Just take some time to take it slow. Don't worry about how you want it to work out for you and how fast you would like things to go because you want to accomplish something that is so important in your daily life. Even if you want the future to be brighter just believe in yourself and trust yourself to reach those goals. Don't be afraid to want to get everything done because you think that if you don't then things won't be how you wanted them to turn out to be. Just realize something, you are the one who is in charge of your life and the goals you want to reach, you will reach them if you put your trust into them and give it time. Everything in this world takes time and sometimes it takes the longest time just so things will work out for the best in the end. Why should you worry so much about things? Stop worrying and just trust that what you want will happen the way you want it to go. When you trust yourself instead of worrying, the outcome is always positive and never negative. You are not going to want to put yourself through stress all day long worrying about the future. It will only cause you to end up with more distractions in your life. So, take my advice and focus on what you want and what you would like to do but don't be so quick to get it done. Some women worry about themselves and say, well everyone else is moving forward why is it taking me forever to get to the place I want to be? Some women say, why is it taking me so long to do the things that I want to get done in my life? Well, let me you something that I think you ought to know. Who cares about what another person has going on in their life? You shouldn't worry about what they are doing and what they have going on in their life because what they have going on in their life is there business. You shouldn't worry about what they do or what they are going to do. Just stay focus on yourself and if you want things to work out for you in your life. When you have all the faith in your goals or whatever it is that you want to get done then you know that you are really trying to make something out of yourself. Don't ever bring yourself down for what other women may have because what they have may not be what makes you happy. Only you can determine what is going to make you happy as a person and what it is that you would like to do and continue to do in your life. Many women feel like they have to rush. Some women even find themselves competing with other women just to prove to them that they are better than them even if it is not true. Some women think because they have more than others it's ok to hurt other people. Well the fact of the matter is that only you can tell yourself that you are not that same person who used to care about what other people may have thrown at you because you learned how to get passed every situation and learned how to deal with it in a positive matter. For everyone women out there who has been hurt or felt hurt, remember you are a woman of great strength. If someone is trying to prove you wrong or trying to compete with you then you know it's because they don't trust themselves at all. They already have lost confidence in themselves. They are just trying to bring you down with them but you have to take control and say "I will not let what you say or do effect my plans for my life." In that very moment, you have made the enemy just lose all power over you. Take some time to begin to realize what you already wanted to do with your life and how you set your goals and your ideas ahead of everything else that has been happening to you. Turn your focus and your attention on yourself. Stop trying to look at other people's plans or their lives because you don't even know if what they are doing is truly what makes them happy. Some women just have things in their life but that doesn't mean they're happy because of what they are doing. Once you focus on yourself and see things in your own perspective, then you come to realize you are beginning to change your lifestyle and become a great woman of confidence. Never be afraid to do new things in your life. It is ok to change your mind but if it's constantly a change of plans then you need to slow it down and come to realize what it is that you really want to do exactly. You are only going to confuse yourself at the end. Stay focus and positive in all of your ideas and when you feel like you need some time to rest then rest. When you are rushing to get something done so fast things get messed up and don't really go as you planned them. So, just look at your life. Be proud that you have made it this far in life and can move on to the next level. Every woman should be able to have the career that they want in life and nobody should stand in their way from getting it. You are your own woman; you make your own decisions. Never let anyone make decisions for you because they don't run your life, you do. You are in control of your own life and what you do is what you want to do. Believe what you do is what makes you a successful person. When you start to take control of your life and not let anyone take control of your life for you, then you'll see you are becoming stronger not just as a person but as a woman who can stand on her own feet and not be discouraged about what others think or say to you to make you feel less than perfect. Even if you do make mistakes when you're trying to do something you should continue and never give up on yourself. It's ok because we all make mistakes. That's where we learn how to overcome them and not turn around and do the same things we did in the past. Why should you doubt yourself for one minute? Why should you be afraid to do the things you want to do? Is it because someone said you would never be able to complete your plans or achieve your dreams? Then guess what, you are making them win over your life if you actually believe what they are saying to you is true. When you start to do what it is that you want to do and give yourself the strength to do it, you just gave yourself the power to be a woman of great confidence. You are a woman with great confidence when you reach up to your decisions in life and go through with them. Even if you feel like they are so hard, you are always going to go through some rough times to get through your goals in life. Don't just give up; continue to do what you wanted to do. You are in control. Don't ever bring yourself down, not even a little bit because things might be so hard to do. Take it one step at a time and continue to work with it and you will accomplish everything you have been planning to do in your life. Only you have the ideas and dreams. Only you can do them the way you feel that they should be done. Only you can empower yourself to get through it and to prove to yourself that you made it. Your life has more meaning then you ever thought. You are your own person who will learn how to handle your situations by continuing and never turning around because that is the first step of failure. Why should you fail to do what you want to do? People's opinions of how you live your life or how you want to live your life, is none of their business. Remember, what others say to affect you doesn't matter if you don't let it. People are always going to keep on nagging at you when they see what you got going on that is making you truly happy. Don't just give up because they are making you tired. Instead, prove to yourself not to them because you don't ever have to prove anything to anybody. What they think about your life is not their business. Prove to yourself that you can do anything you set your mind to. Your life is the only thing that should matter to you. When you move pass the pain, negative talk and torture of hurtful words then you realize you will begin to tell yourself, "hey nothing that any of these things that people are throwing at me is bothering me anymore." Let me tell you why. You passed on to a whole new level and a whole new passage in your life. You have given yourself the faith to be motivated in all that you wanted to accomplish. Always take your time to do things that you are doing. Set the time for everything and let things go with the flow and watch how you will see the things you have been wanting come true. Your life is the most important thing you should know. It is your life you should love it and embrace it every step of the way. A woman who can get past her fears and move forward in her past is a woman with a great force of strength. You should never allow yourself to be scared of someone trying to empower you and confuse you so much that they will block your path in life. You must be the one who will find that path and follow it even if it takes a while to get it all done the way you would like it to be done. When I say "every woman should empower herself", I don't mean to walk around saying "hey, I have the power am winning". No, what I am saying is believe in yourself, tell yourself you are in control of your own abilities in life. Focus on your own path rather than focusing on others. Don't ever try to look at other people's plans. Stay on your road and keep on going until you reach the success line. You are the answer to your own question. When you think that you need to say "hey am I doing the right thing"? Remember you are. You are in the right path if you continue to walk in that same path every day. Miracles don't happen overnight and dreams don't come true until you wake up from them but when you work hard for what you want and what you would like to have for yourself, then you will be so proud that you succeeded with all of your plans. Never turn around from something that you started. Keep on going until the end and when you do, you will be the happiest woman alive. You will be so proud of yourself for keeping your mind set on all of your plans that you have always wanted to do. You are a woman who can do all things. Trust in yourself and you can accomplish your dreams in no time. When you come to the point where you have reached all of your plans and you have success, then you will be amazed at your own accomplishments and know you are a woman of great self-esteem.

CHAPTER 6

WHY ME?

Many women always question themselves when there with a friend, relative or even alone when so much bad has occurred in their life they can't help but ask. Why do these bad things keep on happening to me when I have been a positive person? It's not that you did anything wrong that these bad things happened. Sometimes these things occur in life but it doesn't mean it won't ever get better. When you do focus on them so much you only begin to get yourself so depress more and more every day. "I don't want you to feel like it's not ok to talk about your feelings with someone if you need to because sometimes that is the best thing in life to get past your deepest emotions." Holding on to your feelings only makes matters worst. Eventually, you will tend to explode because you kept everything locked up inside for so long. When you need to ask questions about your life and don't have the answers to them maybe, seeking help is the best way for you to overcome your biggest issues in life that keep on reoccurring. There is nothing to be ashamed about seeking help from someone else. It's better to get the help and advice from a complete stranger. The reason for that being said is because sometimes when you talk to your family they laugh at you or sometimes when you talk to your friends they don't take you so serious. The best thing to do is to just talk to a complete stranger. I am not saying hey, just walk up to anybody in the street and start expressing your emotions to them. I mean seek help from a therapist who can help you get through your biggest fears that keep on holding you back in life. Don't be afraid to lift yourself up and get the help you need don't let someone else overshadow your life by making you think that the past is still living in you daily life today. You can get pass your past by living a new life and beginning a new way for yourself. Why? Is the biggest question many women keep on saying to themselves and most women never really fully come to the point to understand what happened to them? Even when you feel like you are so confused about things and can't get over it you need to find a way to try to overcome it. Now here is the question I am going to ask you. Why should you put yourself through so much heartache when you been through it in the past? Why would you want to keep on reliving it? There are plenty of ways for women to overcome their biggest issues in life. It all begins with you; if you're willing to seek the help that you need to help you face your biggest problem that you think is still disturbing you till this day. Then you should get the help. Many women say well am not going to seek help because I don't need someone else telling me how to get through in life. Some women may even say well why should, I talk to a stranger about my personal life with them when I don't even know them. Why would I want them to help me? I can get pass it on my own. Well maybe you can, if you feel like you are strong enough to deal with every issue one at a time but the truth is if you get the help it will probably be best for you to overcome your problem quicker. You will have a better understanding of why those things that happened to you affected you so much and continue to affect you. Don't let you fear stand in your way because once you say you won't get the help or don't want to hear anything about it you are only blocking yourself in your own life. Now am going to ask you why would you do that to yourself? Is it because you feel like it's too hard for you to do? Well I will tell you the truth it is not that hard at all to get the past emotions fixed now in the presence moment. That's what makes you an amazing woman not being afraid to get the help you so much need in your life. It is truly important for you to stand your ground and help yourself move past anything that needs to be fixed. The main thing is that I want to tell woman all over the world that every woman should know it is never too late for you to start your life over again. Never be terrified of the future because of what happened to you in the past. Now as I recall many woman feel so neglected that they sometimes don't want to move on not because they don't want to but because they are so afraid to. Listen to me very carefully it is your life why should you let someone else run it for you, take control of your own life now. Remember, you are your own woman what you want in life matters. Don't ever be twisted by lies that anyone might try to throw at you. "You can get through it continue to tell yourself I am going to get pass all of this pain and confusion that I carry with me in my heart." Learn to let it go rather than keep on holding on to that pain that you carry with you every single day. Pain should not be part of your life only happiness, love and joy. Many women find themselves feeling like they can't get through the good in life that they want to reach because the past pain has truly left them scared. Why would I need to do anything to improve my life my life is basically what it is and will never get better? Why should I even try to get help? Most women question these two things every day. Now am going to tell you why wouldn't you want to get help why? Why would you want to continue to think about something so badly that happened to you? It may be a really bad memory that you won't ever forget but that doesn't mean your life is what it used to be or supposed to be. You can build up all of your self-esteem and begin by telling yourself, "this is my life a new day begins with me wanting it to get better." Starting over is "ok actually, it is the best solution to all of your problems that you may have thought you could of never get out of. You are stronger than anything than anyone has ever done to you. When you seek for help you begin by giving yourself trust you believe that you will have a second chance in your life. The person that will speak to you will help you come to terms with every aspect and you will see how things start to change for you each and every day. Remember, it won't happen overnight but slowly and one step at a time. You will start to see your life begin to change. The only thing that you should question yourself every day is why should I hold back on myself in life? "I am worth more than anything my life is as precious to me like a gemstone." "I am going to prove to myself that the past did not win it lost. I won because I learned how to carry on in my life with no shame but with Confidence of the woman I am and the woman I would like to become one day." When you see yourself beginning to move forward and giving yourself that self-trust that you can get past all of your pain then you start to really begin to grow as a person in a more common way. Don't worry about being afraid to get help in the beginning it's practically normal to feel scared. Once, you keep on going on with your plans of seeking help you start to realize that you are improving in so many ways. Remember, you are worth it. Encourage yourself not be afraid to live every moment with a new chapter to your story stay true to who you are. When things seem hard and you don't know what to do just be proud of yourself that you took yourself to a whole new level of having someone to speak to. When, you reach the point of a whole new outlook in life then you will start to tell yourself, "hey I really did it I got over the past with making myself strong enough to get past it." These are the things you should do when you see yourself improving get a piece of paper or a notebook and write down all of the new things that have occur in your life since the past. It will help you to see how much you overcame and how much you grew as a woman. Continue, to keep on writing good things down and when you start to feel a little sad you can go to a quiet place, open up your book and read what it is that you have wrote about yourself improving. When you start to do this you are showing yourself that you have been able to conquer all bad and the results of that came out to be good. You are a very powerful woman who can stand up for herself and get past anything if you put your trust in yourself. It all begins by trusting yourself to get past anything that you need or want to get past. You are your own person whatever the past was like for you in the past just remember; the past is completely over only the presence exists to you now in this time of your life. Don't worry about anything and don't stress yourself out by thinking constantly about things over and over again because believe me it will do you no good. Starting over again just because something bad has happened to you in your life doesn't mean that you should punish yourself for it. It wasn't your fault so don't be so angry at yourself for whatever, has happened to you. Every day, begin by learning new routines so you don't end up back in the same old pattern that you were in. Start, stating good facts about yourself and when you speak to someone who can help you. Tell them everything that you want to say express yourself because that person that you are talking to will be there to help you and they are listening to you because they truly want to help you out and overcome your biggest fear's in life. Begin, by trusting the person that you are talking to that you are seeking help from. Think about yourself in life because, that's what matters the most that is when you know you want to help yourself out you want to do better for yourself. You are a woman who can do all good things in life even when a lot of pain was in your heart. Remember, overcome it. Overcome it and help yourself get past it, don't be in such a rush to say no to help because if you do that is the biggest mistake you can ever possibly make in your life. Your life is so important. You only have one life so live each day with a positive attitude. Believe me at the end of your help you will be a brand new person with a whole different attitude about yourself and the aspects of life. It all begins with you trusting yourself and wanting to get that help to get over the past.

CHAPTER 7

DETERMINATION

Women who have come to realize what they have been through they already stated to themselves that they have the victory. They won, they may have struggled but they survived through all of the hard times. I give a lot of credit to women who have walk away from abusive relationships. They truly are empowering to do that. It takes real strength and most of all courage. When you know you have gotten past the things that were making you feel less than a woman or just not being able to get through in life and then you see yourself come to a new path that is because you were the one who sacrifice so much to get to the place where you are today. You should know that you stand stronger than you once did. Your life is yours and you have taken all of that hurt and learned how to deal with it as a responsible Woman. Shame on any man who has ever abused a woman. Shame on them, they are less than a man and they will never fully come to understand who they are as a person because they only think of themselves. They don't seem to have a heart for anyone but for the women who walk through it out alive. God bless you because you are a woman who has told a story that only you will remember for a lifetime. You are the flower to your seed. You have shown so much improvement by turning your life around. You have done all that with one word, "trust". You trusted yourself to get passed it and you did. You believed that you were going to be in a better place and on a better path. What you did to stay alive and to be strong was an amazing opportunity for you because you saw that you had many more things in life to accomplish. You were strong to stick to them and get through them without telling yourself that you couldn't make it. You really should be proud of yourself. You gave yourself so much inspiration to do better for yourself. It's never worth it to stay in a hurtful relationship, what's the point when someone is abusive? They won't ever stop their ways until they get help. Sometimes getting help still doesn't change them. As for women who lived through it and got out alive, just know you are the true fighter who has won the fight. Your life may have been hell in the past but you changed it around and you are living in perfect peace because you showed yourself that you had more courage than the pain that you were experiencing. Many women can actually speak about their past pain and not be embarrassed and that's what makes them realize they are strong. Some women don't ever look back and just continue on with their life and act as if that part of their life never happened. Every woman will react different to their pain and the truth is, "it is ok". As long as you feel comfortable with what you feel you need to do or should do. You should be able to feel free to express yourself because you are your own woman of great faith. With that being said, you did all that you could to get to the place where you stand today. Why shouldn't you be the same person you were in the past? The truth is you are always going to be the person you were and always intended to be but with a little effort and some work you will become past that experience. You will be proud of yourself and you're going to make a new path in your life and not let any man confuse you ever again. You know better not to fall into the same road you were in. You've learned so much and how to get on with your own life. When you passed on to a new level, you were also changing as a woman. You are a woman who lives with self-freedom. That is the key to a confident woman being able to do what you want to do, when you want to do it without being abused by no man or any person. You have made it and keep on following the path that you want to follow. Whatever it is that you set for yourself in life, get it done with great expectations of yourself. Remember, every woman who has ever been in a hurtful past will overcome it with her own true strength. No one can make you change unless you are willing to change for yourself and for the better of your future. What you want to do in your life is the most amazing thing you can ever want. Don't ever let anyone tell you different. Some women have come to a point in their lives where they have reached their goals and some women come to a point where they are working so hard to get to their goals. Whatever it is that you do, just remember you have to have the passion to do the things that you love to do because if you don't then you'll just end up giving up on yourself. Why would you want that when you've come this far in life? Only you can allow yourself to be a woman with great strength and say, "I will do what I want to do and continue to work the best I can." You see, every woman has their own thing going on and when they come to realize that this is what's making them truly happy then they become happy. When you learn how to live up to your own expectations and above all you are rising in a new path when you don't give in to the horrible experience that was behind you and you learned how to move forward, you are truly staying positive as a woman. Now when I said "every woman should define who they are and not let anyone define them", what I meant by that is you should look forward to what you have going on in your life and do what you want to do without being so afraid of the past. When you learn that you are your own person and others can't define you then you come to an agreement that you are stronger than any other person has said or done to you. You begin to go with a new flow and follow yourself to a better path in your life.

Some women are truly insecure after an abusive hurtful past but that doesn't mean that it happened overnight in their lives but most women were determine to help themselves get passed whatever it was that they needed to passed. They truly are an inspiration to other women who have gone through the same experience. Some women can relate to them on so many levels. Well, some women begin with a new attitude of themselves and looking back at the person who hurt them with themselves not be ashamed but leaving the abuser with no power. When you continue your life and look back at it, you are giving the person that hurt you not even a little bit of self-control over your life. You are winning in your life because you are showing yourself how you have set a new path in front of you and you will not let anyone take that away from you. "You are your own person", I will keep on repeating this line because some women don't believe that after an emotional break through. When you been through the pain remind yourself on a daily bases, "that was me then and this is me now. I am not the same person I use to be and I will never be that same person who was so afraid to move on because I thought less of myself." That is what you need to remind yourself because what you have going on in your life is an amazing thing that you should be proud of. You have made it this far without anyone getting in your way. I want to explain this to every women in the world, when you do something you really feel like you should do and you fail the first time, then the second time and then third that doesn't mean you failed as a person it means at that moment when you were doing the things you wanted to do but couldn't reach those goals it wasn't time for you to be in that place and it wasn't meant to be for you to have. Maybe it's just that you need more time before you can go through with it because you weren't ready for it as a person. That doesn't make you less than a woman and it certainly doesn't make you a failure. You are not a failure. Only failing when you don't try for the better, that's when most women feel like they are losing hope in themselves. Never give up if you failed. Try it again and if it still doesn't work out try something else that you would like to do in your life. Believe me, it is not the end of the world. Don't be so hard on yourself. Don't exaggerate every situation. Just continue with new things and go from there. You are an empowering woman who can do the most valuable things that you want to do. Most of what you do in your life is up to you and no one else's business. It is your choice. Don't ever think you need to explain yourself to anyone. Just to do the things that mean the most to you in your life. By moving with your plans to a whole new level, you are improving as a woman who knows what she wants and is not afraid to go after it. Treat yourself with love in all that you do and the results of your life's outcome will be as pleasant as you can ever imagine. You are a woman with great strength, you stand with great confidence when you move past those bitter lies and not get yourself twisted or confuse with what rumors may have been said about you. When you learn not to care what people think, then you are growing with more power and more self-esteem in your life. Life is just so beautiful and there are so many wonderful things you can do with your life. Never let anyone tell you different. What you want and what you would like to do, you will make it will great motivation passed your fears. You are strong and growing stronger everyday once you learn how to take control of yourself. No one controls you, no one but you. When you look back at the past and see yourself in the place that you are in right now, then you will say to yourself "wow did I really get through this? Am I really in this place that I always wished to be in?" The results will be "yes". With your belief, you gave yourself the best opportunity anyone could ever have in their life. Not giving up. You have done what you wanted to do. Don't think you did it because you were doing it with a little bit of faith. You were doing it with courage and because you encouraged yourself through the whole path and you never once said "you know what? I think am going to give up hope." You kept on going and that's what has made you a woman with a whole new positive outlook in life. You have truly seen that you are a woman of courage who has faced your biggest fears in life.

CHAPTER 8

RESPECT

Now is the time to stand up for your-self and say enough is enough. The past is over I am a new person. Anyone that enters my life will not bring me down. I will not tolerate nonsense from anyone, no man will abuse me with his words and nobody will make me fall apart because I learn how to show myself that I truly love myself. No man is worth pain and no one who enters my life will throw me down to the same path that I was once in because I learn how to live as a person and not be treated like dirt. I want the same respect that I would have to give out and if any man or any person doesn't respect me then I will just take them out of my life and not let them have any part of my life because I will not bring myself back down that same path in life that I was once in. Many women have been through pain, abuse, torture even thrown out of there house because of fights with their lovers. Well here is the time to start right. Once you stand back up with your own two feet and you begin to fully understand that you have grown and got past all of that you have been through, and then you will only learn how to tolerate respect for yourself. If someone doesn't respect you then why should you keep on holding on to them in your life? They will never come to give you the respect you want because, they don't care about you. The truth is they don't care about themselves so why should they care about anyone else. When someone cares about you or has feelings for you or even loves you they will treat you with the same respect that they would want to be treated. Women who feel abused. "GET OUT" and don't stay with someone who will bring you down all of the time or crack jokes about you. You need to come to know that you are a woman who tolerates her respect and that should be you're first thing on your list. What I want every woman to know is that what you want and what you believe is right. What you want in your life is important to you and no one should interfere with what it is that you want in your life. With that being said, whoever thinks that they have power over you they don't and don't ever think that you should allow that person to be part of your life. It all comes down to having a certain amount of respect and most women don't get the respect they deserve because, of a lot of nonsense and rumors that are being said about them. It's not there place to say something about you but, you know we live in a world where people are always going to run their mouth and never stop when they see that what you have going on for yourself is good. What you need to do is just make sure you never give in to their words as being the truth. Stand up for yourself show yourself some respect damn it you deserve all the respect you can get. Some women will say "well it's ok if people don't want to respect me. I can live with that". No! You should not let that be said and done to yourself the reason for that being said is because you need to protect your reputation as a woman. If you let anyone disrespect you then they think that they have power over you and that they can say whatever they want about you whenever they want. Don't let that be the cause. Remember, you should have the same respect any other person may want. Why should any other person think that they have the permission to empower themselves over your life? "No" one should be that afraid to let someone run their mouths and just start saying awful hurtful words. Just like they wouldn't like that being said and done to them that's exactly how you should feel about yourself. Remind, yourself if am not being treated with respect then you need to get out of my life and stay out because I will not want any part of that in my life. I am at a better place in my life and whatever is going on in my life is my own thing whatever people say about me is a lack of childish immaturity that's when you know you have grown as a woman and the person running their mouth will always be the same person they once were. It all comes down to respect you should always make someone give you respect whether it is a male or a female. "WHEN YOU SAY YOU WANT RESPECT, MEAN IT BECAUSE YOU WILL GET IT!" Most women don't care. The truth is you should care. Its apart of also having respect for yourself. You as a woman, don't ever let anyone treat you with cruelty because believe me they wouldn't want you to treat them like that. Always keep this number one fact to have respect you must give respect. Women who have been hurt in the past just because of a bad relationship or an abusive one feel like they lose all of their confidence and don't know how to regain that respect that they once lost. You have to be in charge of yourself and tell any man that disrespects you exactly who you are as a woman and what you expect in return from a man. Don't let a man tare your abilities down. Don't let anyone tare you down or what you have rebuilt and worked so hard in your life for. Your life is your number one thing and without giving yourself respect it is like saying, "hey anybody can just walk all over me." When you learn how to stick up for what you believe in and don't let no one mistreat you then you are standing up to your ability as a woman with confidence and believing in yourself to get that respect that you need. If you begin a new relationship with anyone, even a friend, make sure you know that they treat you with an amount of respect because, you don't want to have someone in your life like who will make you feel like you are not worth it. As a matter of fact some woman instantly feels like they can learn from their past mistakes quickly. You should learn how to stand up for yourself and not let anyone tell you how your life is supposed to be or shouldn't or that you're making the wrong choices. It's your life and your future nobody who has bad words against you are truly the people you can't trust they are more like I can say the person who is trying to make you feel like a failure. Remember, stand yourself to a higher level and make others realize that you want to be treated with respect. When someone can't be positive to you in your life then what is the point of staying with them. When someone doesn't give you respect why bother being with them cut them out of your life and don't regret it because, they are not worth it. You don't need that abuse in your life. Your life is about adding goodness to it and not bad. Why should you allow someone to hurt you so bad and continue to have them stay in your life? If someone is like that towards you, does that mean it gives them the right to put pain back into your life? My answer to that question is, absolutely not. You are an amazing woman when you stand up to your beliefs and come to a point to say I have been down this road and I will not allow it to enter my life and affect me anymore. The main focus is if a man can't respect you, he will never respect you because he obviously doesn't care about you or your feelings. Get pass that just like you have already had in your life. Believe me there are other men in this world that are willing to love you, respect you and want to respect your wishes. When you least expect the goodness to come to your life think again because there is someone out there better for you and who is willing to listen to what you have to say. Respect is your first priority and you need to never forget that. Why should you think that a controlling man will ever change his ways. That is not going to happen because they don't have respect for themselves. Any man who is willing to destroy a woman's life already has been destroyed by his own life. He will never come to fully give you respect so you must not tolerate his nonsense and learn how to be a woman with power, great strength and get up and walk away. Move on with yourself. Give yourself credit for what you do because you deserve it. You worked hard to accomplish what you want in your life and who is any-body to come in the way and mistreat you. Let them know that they will not have that control over you. Your life begins with you taking over every situation that has tried to harm you. You are in charge of your future. Your ability of containing respect does matter. Don't let anyone twist that around for you. When you want someone in your life, give them a chance to listen to what you want. You never know, the person you may be speaking with may even relate to you in so many ways. They might even be there to help you with some great guidance. Not everyone that is in your life is going to give you respect but those that do are the ones that are trying to be there in your life. Maybe to be your friend, maybe to be with you in a relationship. Like I said before, when someone doesn't give you the respect you want and mistreats you the best thing to do is to get them out of your life. Why put up with them? What are you gaining by allowing them to speak to you in anyway? You are actually losing control of yourself when you let someone step all over you. Why should you let them distract you? You have so much to offer life. Don't let it be taken away from you with the word of envy from someone else. What they want to say about you is just them being so upset with themselves that they don't know how to reach a new path in life for themselves. You should never see yourself as what they are describing to you or saying to you because it is not true at all. As long as you know who you are as a woman and what you want then learn how to live it that way each day. Don't let the past ruin your status of who you ought to become. Today live up to your highest value. Follow your path that you were continuing to follow and don't stop for once for anybody. Remember, you have to give yourself respect if you want others to respect you. If you don't, what makes you think they will? Only you can love yourself and prove to yourself that you are not a person who will tolerate anybody's words abusing you with their lies. You are stronger than they can ever picture you being. You are a woman who will demand her respect and earn her respect. You are a woman who is always going to have that self-respect regardless of what anyone says or thinks about you. Your life is important to you and so are your values so live with that self-respect and don't ever change for anyone and don't ever let anyone take that away from you. Respect, that's what you will have in your life as a woman of confidence.

CHAPTER 9

FORGIVENESS

I think the most important thing in a person's life is forgiveness I mean how can you get pass all of the pain if you don't find it in your heart to forgive. Forgiving, doesn't mean you have to ever talk to that person again it just means you found a way to let go of what they did or may have done to you." It's like you are letting yourself be forgiven by forgiving whatever, it is that may have happened to you. Some Woman will say, Well how can I forgive someone who did so much wrong to me? Some woman may even say why should I forgive the person who has abused me so much? I'll tell you why you should forgive them. When you forgive them you are taking all of the hurt inside of you and letting it go you are embracing yourself to show yourself that you love yourself so much to let go of the pain that you had stored inside of you for so long. Why should you keep on thinking about what someone did to you in the past they are not worth it, if you keep on going back to that over and over again then you're not living life. You're making them live there life while you stay miserable because, of what someone did to you and it just keeps on eating you up every single day so the hell with them move on just give yourself a break from what you have been through because of them. Once, you just start letting go a little at a time you will see your life will start to be much better, whatever they did to you forgive them for the sake of yourself. Learn to forgive I am not saying you will ever forget or want to be close to that person but just forgive because with that being said forgiveness is the only thing that helps you heal the most in your life for yourself and not anybody else. What will you gain out of holding on to a grudge with someone who has done you wrong? If you don't know? Then you ought to know, nothing because whatever someone has done to you even if it they hurt you to your soul you don't gain anything by not forgiving them it only makes you angrier every single day you just start to bring a negative force to yourself. Why should you be living like that when the person that has hurt you moved on and didn't care what thy done to you? "It's because, a lot of foolishness and sometimes immaturity don't let their immaturity make you immature as a woman." When you forgive someone it doesn't mean you have to go up to that person and say I forgive you for everything you done to me, but some woman empower themselves to do that. That's when you come to a point in your life that you know you are really Confident. Well anyway, when you do forgive someone who has hurt you, you are proving to yourself that you are stronger than any words that they have said to make you felt less than perfect. Forgiving is the best thing you can do for yourself to help you move on in your life. It is the only things you can do to make yourself a stronger person what I mean but that is when you forgive someone who did you wrong you learn how to take the pain and turn it into a positive solution. Remember, your life is the most important part of living so why live with so much anger from the past if you don't let go then you're not moving pass anything in your life everything you do is going to affect you. When you feel like you don't know how to forgive someone give yourself some time to think about why that person that hurt you did what they did to You. Don't lower yourself to anybody's level just because, someone did wrong to you. It doesn't mean you need to go and do wrong to them. Believe me it's not going to solve anything but only makes matters worst. Learn how to stay calm when you battle a heavy situation with someone because, if you just keep on telling yourself you will not be the one to be overwhelmed by what another person has done to you. You are forgiving for the sake of yourself; you are beginning to help yourself grow as a Woman who can learn to overcome anything that may have happened to you in your life. Forgiveness is a big key to self-healing for all those who don't know that you must forgive to move forward. Once you have forgiven the person who has hurt you, you will be impress with yourself because, you won't believe how strong enough you truly was to get pass that situation. Sometimes, in life the people that you learn to forgive end up becoming your closest friends and sometimes they may come to a point in their life were they feel like they made mistakes towards you too. Not everyone is going to have the same respond to forgiveness but, for some people they may look at it from a different point of view. Just remember, what you are feeling. If you are moving forward in life but find some resentment or anger and feel like it's always like that for you in your daily life the reason for that being said is that you need to learn how to forgive the past to and to overcome it. There are many reasons why someone can say what they say to hurt someone maybe, its jealousy anger, self-hatred wanting what the other person may have. But if you are a bigger person then you will be the one to say ok I will forgive them for all of the wrong that they have done or said to me. Sometimes hurtful words can be said because, they are so hurt that they are taking their anger on someone else and don't even realize that they hurting another person so much because they never really stop to think what they did to that person. So here is your chance to change what you use to feel and bring in a new fresh positive attitude to your life. When you forgive someone and truly mean that forgiveness all of the pain that you held inside of you will feel like you have just remove a hot air balloon from your chest, what I mean by that is that you will feel like you have just released so much tension that you were holding on inside of you. Every woman should know that anger is not good for your soul and the more anger you hold on to the harder it is for you to ever let any of it go. Let the pain of what someone did you be released from your soul by just forgiving them remember, we are all humans we all make mistakes it wouldn't be right to hold on to a grudge for someone for the rest of their lives. "You can be the wiser person and say you know what I know what they did to me wasn't right but, hey I can't live my whole life thinking about how horrible they have made me feel because, that's not going to make me feel better it's not going to erase what that person did to me. So from there on you need to learn how to forgive if you are finding it hard to forgive then speak to someone who can relate to your circumstances and maybe they can help you get past the pain that you are still going through. Sometimes, people do thinks to hurt others and they don't mean it intentionally but it can get out of line and words can hurt really badly only if you let it have that much over you. Another, way to forgive someone who has hurt you is by just taking a piece of paper and writing down everything that person has done to you and remove them out of your list by placing a positive affirmation and see how you feel about that after you are done. Some woman may even journal in their book that is also another great way to express your forgiveness by writing down what you feel. If you are a type of person that wants to forgive someone and wants them to know that you want to forgive them the only last solution is to confront them face to face and tell them that you forgive them for what they have done to you or what they have said about you. If that person is mature to know what they did to you was wrong then they will apologize for hurting you so much but, if not don't get angry because some people never like to admit when were wrong and sometimes they will never grow out of that nonsense. You must be the adult and just remember, forgive to be forgiven and many doors will open for you, knew blessings will come forward in your life. You will start to see yourself growing as a person when you let things go and forgive. You will start to see yourself as a whole new person with a great attitude. Believe in yourself that you can forgive the person that hurt you. When someone does something wrong to you, you got to prove to yourself that what they said to you has no power over you. There words were useless why should you drive yourself crazy with the nonsense that they have made you believe or may have try to make you believe, it's not worth it. When you forgive truly mean it because, there will be some extra pain that you need still need to resolve if you just hold on to all of that pain. Remind yourself to try to build that self-courage you must be willing to let go and move forward to help yourself bring that self-esteem back. Someone may say stupid stuff to make you feel like dirt but, is it true? No then why do you care so much about what they say they are speaking through their own anger and sometimes when you come to a point in your life to forgive them they will realize wow this person truly forgave me. Then they will start to question how come? The truth of the matter is that you know the reason why you found it in your heart to forgive that person. When you see yourself forgiving someone it's like you're forgiving yourself for being so angry all these years for holding on to something that someone has made you feel. It's like you are giving yourself a second opportunity to see pass the bad experiences that you once experience in your life. When you do see yourself forgiving, it will feel like a whole brand new day like as if the sun appeared and all of the dark clouds, thunder and rain have just vanished away. When you do forgive not only are you being forgiven you are healing yourself in so many levels and you will see that the rest of your days will begin to grow with great ambition. You will see that you have improve as a person and come to learn how to grow with true self-esteem you are a person who has great strength ahead of herself you are a confident woman when you find the courage to forgive and all else will be well. "You must believe that what you did you did it for yourself to become, a better woman and that's what you are and that's what you will always be." As a Woman who gave herself a change in life and a better path in her life. "Note to all Woman when you forgive someone you are forgiving yourself for everything you have ever held inside of you."

CHAPTER 10

YOUR DESTINY THE FINAL WORD

So here it is your life your future the beginning of your dreams all coming true. Change is starting to occur in your life new things are starting to happen because; you are making the effort to turn your life around. "You are woman who has so much going on and more." Goodness will come to you as long as you stand up with that positive attitude and continue to focus on the things you want to reach in your life. Remember, you are not just a woman with a past you are a Woman with great potential and so much courage because, you learned how to face your problems instead of running away from them. It all starts with you. The Future is the new pathway for you. Remember, to remain in control of your situation continue to follow your dreams and you will see your destiny unfold like a gift that was wrapped. Your empowering courage is what gives you the strength everyday not to give up on yourself. This is for all women you are worth more than hurtful cruel words they don't mean anything to you unless you give in to it too much. Your life begins with new outcomes and your life is going to be everything you ever wanted it to be. Keep your head held high and continue to go with your ideas they won't fail if you believe in yourself. Your future is going to be everything beautiful and so much more because; you have faith in all that you continue to do. Your dreams are your dreams what you want and am speaking for every Woman in the world what you want is the most valuable thing so don't let no one take it that away from you. You belong to a bright and amazing future which is waiting to be revealed to you in this life time. When you look in the mirror you will be amazed at what you see because, you are a Woman with a new attitude who had a lot of bad going on but, that didn't stop you at all from moving past them to a better spot. Here is my advice to all women. When someone tells you what Confidence is? You should always respond by telling them this. You are looking at a Woman with Courage, Self-Esteem and Self-Love that is what Confidence is and that is what every woman should know what Confidence is about. Here is the thing you should always remember you are an amazing woman with the most amazing ideas. No one can ever stand in your way or mistaken you for what you are and what you will become. "Your dreams are important don't ever back out of them for no one and don't ever let anyone ever back you down for anything you always wanted to do. Your life begins with you saying yes and your future your only new thing that you should be looking forward in life is the future and not the past. The past is over and done with. Don't ever go back, to what could, should or would have been like "it's over" here is where your life starts. Today not tomorrow, not next year but, today this very moment. Think big continue to move with the strength you have inside and use your courage to help you every step of the way. Everything, that I have said in all of my chapters are lessons many woman can learn from and experience of how to overcome them. You see you should just believe that you are worth it and anything in your life that you have to go through sometimes works out for the best because, it helps you reach the place where you stand today. A better place, a new place that you thought you could of never reach. Sometimes you got to go through the roughest things in life to really see how strong of a woman you are. Don't ever fail yourself this is your life you see your life has so much meaning so much more for you to offer just wait and see it's like I said before just be patience it will all work out the way you want it to. Work hard for what you want but the truth is this whatever road you take in life whatever, path you choose your choosing it because, you know it works for you. When things might not go directly as you planned stay calm because, maybe it wasn't meant to be. Take chances in life and if you fail, you just remember you didn't fail as a person. You are a person who wasn't afraid of trying to reach the next level in her life. Give yourself credit for that. You are an amazing Woman and what you are doing is amazing. Keep up the great Confidence in yourself. Your destiny is going to be bright you see you were made to have a plan in life and you will reach those plans in life when the time is right. "The only thing is to never give up." Failure is something, that some woman may choose but think again it will lead you know were in life. Begin with your career and move forward on with your life from there. "I think every woman should have a great career that makes her happy." You have a perfect destiny if you look at yourself and see that you have what it takes to make them come true. No matter, how hard you try and even if things don't turn out the way you thought they would just know there is still something better for you in your life that you still haven't found yet. Everything, that you do everywhere that you go, you are working hard to make it possible for you to work out in your life, so embrace what you are doing with passion. "You have the final word to your life your life" Your life begins with you and not with what people say about you. It begins by what you determine and what you say in your own life. Never, say never, your destiny is in your hands. You begin your future everyday by changing the things that you don't approve of from your past. You start to see yourself beginning with changing things that need to be change and right at that moment you are a woman with power in her life. With that one positive attitude in your life you are creating a new future for yourself. See now here's the time and place when you step up for what you want to do and begin to change the things that you thought you never could of do. Your strength and your beliefs comes from within you which gives you self-confidence as a woman, your courage is within you, every day of your life as you move forward without looking at the past pain you have been through in your life. To get to a better new place in life you must never look back but only ahead of your new goals in your life that you want to achieve. Your future is so bright and full of spark, live in the presence moment with that light in your life. Remember, there is nothing that can make you confuse to moving to the next level because, you are in control of your life, your situation and nothing no one says can stand in your way. Anything you want you will have you have the power to do it because, you have grown to a new level of Self-Trust in yourself and your dreams. You have so much to inspire the world with your talent so go for it, and don't turn you're away from what you believe in doing. "Your heart may have been broken once but the pieces to your cracked heart will become whole again because you can fix it with encouragement, love, patience, courage, self-trust and always Self-Esteem in yourself. Nothing bad lasts forever and your heart will not be broken forever. For all women out there I want you to know that life does get better, you do get past all of it and you do see that one day you will turn back and remember what I wrote in this book that came true for you. You are a Self-Confident Woman who can dream bigger than anything. A women who can reach for the stars even in the most painful way. Remember, you determine your future your life begins with you by just making a change and always believing in yourself and not what anyone has to say to you. "When you look in the mirror you will see yourself as a Woman who has changed in a more beautiful way and you will be so proud every day to say hey "I am so beautiful" and you should say that to yourself once a day." Every woman should encourage herself with calling herself beautiful not only from the outside but also from the inside. You have so much to offer the world with your great extreme talent. Only with that confidence that you carry every day you will achieve it. You must stay focus on yourself. Continue to do what you planned to do in your life with great Confident. "You are a Woman who has learned how to control your emotions and you should always tend to keep them that way because, you know how great your future will be for you and what lies ahead for you in the new path that you take in your life. A Woman who has passed her past without ever thinking about it and just looking ahead to where she wants to be is a Woman who is giving herself a second chance in her life, a woman who is trying to open new doors in her life and see a new outcome for her in her life. When someone is knocking on your door to bring you down you can just slam that door and open a new one." Remember, you don't and you won't ever let yourself go through what you been through from before. If something in your life isn't working out the way you want it its ok try something new something different. It might be a better path for to have in life. Here is my advice to all Women all over the world remember, you were so strong to get past all the pain and heartache and you have made it this far so go on with yourself. See, how much ability you have with your life and all the good that can come with it along the way. What you want to achieve is your goals and it's because you determine what you want in life never let anyone determine what you want to do in your life. Your life belongs to you and you alone. You have the final word to your life see the things you want and go for it. When you come to reach a whole new level it's because, of the courage that you have had with you along the way. "Don't ever fade away the pain but embrace it with something positive that will make your future your beginning of your life. Your life Is your life and what you want to happen will happen if it's meant to be, just believe that it will and remember everybody has their own true destiny in life. "Your life is not over it is just the beginning. So here it is to the entire Wonderful Woman in the World. You are brave, strong independent and full of great potential. You are an empowering woman with great confident who has learned the value of Love Respect and Dreams. "Your future your destiny already begins in this very moment."